I Can Have What I Say
Book Series

Everyday Prayers for
Adults

L. Toy Pridegon

WHAT YOU SAY PUBLISHING

I Can Have What I Say Book Series

Everyday Prayers for Adults

© 2023 L. Toy Pridegon

Published by WHAT YOU SAY Publishing

ISBN 979-8-9881437-2-7

Unless otherwise indicated, all Scripture taken from Bible Gateway Public Domain. No permission necessary.

Printed in the United States

10 9 8 7 6 5 4 3 2 1

For Worldwide Distribution

All Scriptures used came from:

- Amplified Bible (AMP)

- Amplified Bible, Classic Edition (APMC)

- King James (KJV)

- New Living Translation (NLT)

- The Message Bible (MSG)

- Evangelical Heritage Version (EHV)

- English Standard Version (ESV)

- The Living Bible (TLB)

- The Voice (Voice)

DEDICATION

The prayers written in this book have been written so you can experience and maintain success in every area of your life.

God wants you to know Him intimately, He wants you to know that you can and should come to Him in good times and bad, whether or not you've walked in obedience to Him or messed up big time. He wants you to always come boldly to the Throne of Grace in prayer. He wants you to come and pray to the Father in Jesus Name.

PREFACE

Each book in the "I Can Have What I Say" book series is to be used as a tool to: teach the prayer warrior how to pray accurately and with specificity; build confidence; increase your faith; help you to patiently endure as you wait for the manifestation of your prayers that by faith have already been answered.

ACKNOWLEDGMENTS

I would, of course, like to thank God for leading me and giving me the strength to write this, my fifth book in the series of I Can Have What I Say books. As I wrote the prayers, I was reminded of many things I've gone through myself or help others prayer through.

I would also like to thank my family, who through the many circumstances we've faced together, brought me to my knees in prayer and taught me how to wait patiently for the manifestation of the answers I believed God for.

Last but certainly not least I would like to thank my husband who has always supported me. His unconditional love, patience, discernment and prayers keep me grounded, focused and able to accomplish much in the kingdom of God.

TABLE OF CONTENTS

ENTER INTO THE PRESENCE OF GOD

TAKE CARE OF YOU

VICTORY

THE WORKPLACE

THE BODY OF CHRIST

GOVERNMENT – COMMUNITY BUSINESS

FAMILY

PERSONAL GROWTH

INTRODUCTION

Prayer is saying things that haven't happened yet, a speaking those things that are not real yet as if they were real right now. Your mind won't want you to say such things because it almost feels like you're lying, but NO! You are speaking words filled with faith. You are behaving like God wants you to, speaking His language. Now you are walking by faith and not by sight. Soon your heart will believe the words your mouth speaks and your ears hear. He hears you and rest assured He is going to make sure your prayer, which is according to His will for you, shall come to pass.

Romans 4:17-18 King James Version (KJV**) Speak like you already have the answer.**

[17] (As it is written, I have made thee a father of many nations,) before him whom he believed, even God, who quickeneth the dead, and calleth those things which be not as though they were.

[18] Who against hope believed in hope, that he might become the father of many nations, according to that which was spoken, So shall thy seed be.

Mark 11:23-24 Amplified Bible (AMP) Act like you already have the answer

[23] I assure you *and* most solemnly say to you, whoever says to this mountain, 'Be lifted up and thrown into the sea!' and [a]does not doubt in his heart [in God's unlimited power], but believes that what he says is going to take place, it will be done for him [in accordance with God's will]. [24] For this reason I am telling you, whatever things you ask for in prayer [in accordance with God's will], believe [with confident trust] that you have received them, and they will be *given* to you.

2 Corinthians 5:7 Amplified Bible (AMP) Believe it before you see, feel or hear the answer

[7] for we walk by faith, not by sight [living our lives in a manner consistent with our confident belief in God's promises].

HOW TO USE EVERYDAY PRAYERS FOR ADULTS

1. Simply pray or read the prayers aloud the prayer(s) that are relevant to your life or the lives of others.
2. End each prayer in Jesus Name.
3. Read the scripture reference.

WHAT IS PRAYER

Prayer is asking God to do something for you or on behalf of someone else. It involves speaking and even more listening. You are speaking faith filled words, speaking as if you already have what you are asking for. This is what's called "speaking those things that be not as though they were according to Romans 8:4-17. If you're not used to praying this way it may seem strange at first but remember, you're speaking faith filled words. Your speaking like God speaks. This is how you walk by faith by speaking Gods Word. God will only act on words that line up with His word.

13

WHEN SHOULD YOU PRAY

You should pray every chance you get, I Thessalonians 5:17, King James Version says: Pray without ceasing. The Amplified Bible says: Be unceasing and persistent in prayer. I would suggest that you pick a specific time of day to pray developing a lifestyle of prayer as it becomes a part of your daily routine. Any time and at every opportunity it is a good time to pray, location permitting.

WHERE SHOULD YOU PRAY

You can pray anywhere. In the shower, in your room, on your break at work, at school between classes. No place is off limits unless prayer is not allowed or you would be disruptive or out of order to do so.

HOW LONG SHOULD YOU PRAY

Jesus asked the disciples to pray (Matthew 26:36-40) and rebuked or chastised them when they didn't. Now while this is a good standard to live up to because we are followers of Christ, the most important thing is rather than timing how long you pray it's more important that you are faithful to pray at least once everyday then how long you pray will take care of itself.

WHY SHOULD YOU PRAY

You should pray because we communicate with God this way. You should pray because in life you will be faced with many obstacles, dilemmas and circumstances that God can and will help you with but you must ask by faith through prayer.

WHAT SHOULD YOU PRAY FOR

You can and should pray for whatever concerns you at any given time. Nothing that will ever happen to you, for you or because of you is a surprise to God. So take everything to God in prayer, He wants you to.

TYPES OF PRAYER

1. PRAYER OF THANKSGIVING

The Prayer of Thanksgiving is thanking God for what He has done (Colossians 4:2). It is a good practice to either begin and or end your prayers by giving thanks.

2. PRAYER OF SUPPLICATION

The Prayer of Supplication is when you pray, you can ask God for something for yourself and give Him thanks. Philippians 4:6 says ...by prayer and supplication with thanksgiving you can ask God to do something for you.

3. INTERCESSORY PRAYER

Intercessory Prayer is praying on behalf of others as Abraham did for Sodom and Gomorrah in Genesis 18:23- 34.

4. PRAYER OF WORSHIP

The Prayer of Worship is thanking God for who He is. It is a good practice to either begin and or end your prayers, in addition to giving thanks, with worship as well (Psalm 95:2-3).

5. PRAYER OF CONSECRATION

The Prayer of Consecration is praying to know Gods will (Luke 26:39), Jesus prayed to be assured of Gods will.

6. PRAYER OF IMPORTUNITY

The Prayer of Importunity is a prayer of persistence, to insist on having, will not give up, relentless, consistent. (Luke 11:9)

7. PRAYER OF FAITH

The Prayer of Faith will heal the sick (James 5:15). If you expect to receive an answer to your prayers, then your prayers must be filled with words of faith according to Mark 11:22-25.   Faith Filled Prayers consist of:

17

- Praying according to God's Word
- Believe the prayer you prayed
- Receive the answer before you see the answer by giving God praise
- Act like it's already done

Each prayer in this book contains one or a combination of these prayers. As you become more familiar with prayer and the types of prayer, you'll know which type of prayer you are praying at any given time.

PROLOGUE

I have always heard it said that prayer is simply talking to God just like you would anyone else Prayer doesn't have to be long and drawn out, there is not wrong with long prayer. Prayer doesn't have to be loud but it does have to be spoken. You can talk to God just like you would talk to anyone one else however, you must know what you're talking about. God is waiting to hear you speak faith filed words or else He will not respond. He hastens His word to perform it and is not moved by tears, yes, they are precious and He keeps them but tears alone do not move God but speaking according to His words as you cry does.

PRAYER MUST BE SPOKEN! God spoke the worlds into existence and we must speak what we want as well.

Your confession is your profession so let's get to work.

PRAYER OF PRAISE & THANKSGIVING

Father, I give You thanks and praise today for all the great things You've done for me. I thank You for waking me up today and watching over me as I slept. I thank You for always making a way for me and setting my life on a path of total victory. I thank You for providing for my every need and even granting my Godly heart's desires. Lord, I thank You for loading me up with the benefits of Peace, unconditional Love, Joy and Righteousness. I thank You for Your mercy which never comes to an end but is new every morning.

In Jesus Name! Amen

SCRIPTURE REFERENCE:
Hebrews 13:15 Amplified Bible
Through Him, therefore, let us at all times offer up to God a sacrifice of praise, which is the fruit of lips that thankfully acknowledge and confess and glorify His name.

PRAYER OF WORSHIP

Father, I come to worship You for who You are. I love You, Lord, and magnify Your Name. I appreciate and honor You, Lord. I bless You and give glory to your Name. You are the King of kings and the Lord of lords, the Beginning and the End and I worship You. I magnify You and lift up your Name. I see you high and lifted up and Your train fills the temple. You are my Peace, my Healer, and Deliverer and I worship You. Lord, you are my Provider, my Victory, You are the Most High God, Lord you are worthy of all honor, glory and power. I'll have no other gods before You. You and You only will I worship, honor, adore and serve. **In Jesus Name! Amen.**

SCRIPTURE REFERENCE:
Psalm 95:6 King James Version
O come, let us worship and bow down: let us kneel before the Lord our maker.

CLOSER RELATIONSHIP WITH GOD

Father, I want to be, I need to be closer to You. So I thank You for a closer walk with You. I thank You for the desire to pray more, to read and study the bible more, to worship and praise more. I thank You that as I give You more of me, I'll have more of You. More of Your Peace, Wisdom, Joy, more of everything that You are. Your Word says that when I come close to You, You come close to me.
In Jesus Name! Amen

SCRIPTUREREFERENCE
James 4:8 Amplified Bible
Come close to God [with a contrite heart] and He will come close to you. Wash your hands, you sinners; and purify your [unfaithful] hearts, you double-minded [people].

TO KNOW GOD'S WILL

Father, I thank You that Your Word says I am a wonderful creation and You have made wonderful plans for my life. You knew me before I was born. Your plans for me are good and not evil, to give hope for an amazing future in You. So, I ask You now to reveal Your purpose and those plans for me now, in this season of my life, and I thank You for it.

In Jesus Name! Amen.

SCRIPTURE REFERENCE

Jeremiah 29:11 Amplified Bible

For I know the plans *and* thoughts that I have for you,' says the LORD, 'plans for peace *and* well-being and not for disaster, to give you a future and a hope.

23

COMMAND YOUR DAY

Father, I boldly declare that today is a day of prayer, worship, praise, thanksgiving, victory, favor, success, power, peace, joy, provision, health, safety, purpose, wisdom, growth and freedom. I thank you that today is a great day and I am grateful that my steps are ordered by You and I walk in greatness this day. Today, I am led by your Spirit and goodness and mercy follow me. I thank You Father that today is a day filled with Your presence. I thank You for waking me up to see and participate in this day.

In Jesus Name! Amen.

SCRIPTURE REFERENCE:

Hebrew 11:3 New International Version

[3] By faith we understand that the universe was formed at God's command, so that what is seen was not made out of what was visible.

FAVOR

Father, I thank You that I am highly favored. Your favor that is magnificent, extravagant, extraordinary and lavish, surrounds me like a shield and covers me like a canopy. Your favor opens doors that can not be opened; makes a way out of no way; cancels contracts; changes rules and regulations, hearts and mindsets. Your favor changes no to yes, moves mountains and benefits me daily.

In Jesus Name! Amen

SCRIPTURE REFERENCE:

Psalms 5:12 Amplified Bible, Classic Edition

[12] For You, Lord, will bless the [uncompromisingly] righteous [him who is upright and in right standing with You]; as with a shield You will surround him with goodwill (pleasure and favor).

THE WHOLE ARMOR OF GOD

Father, by faith, I stand before You fully dressed, armed and ready to fight in the spirit, able to stand against anything the Devil sends my way. I wear Truth as a belt and Righteousness as a breast plate. On my feet is the weapon of Peace that walks me through every valley. My Faith is the shield that protects me and my helmet is Salvation, my defense against sickness, poverty and anything that is not like You.

In Jesus Name! Amen.

SCRIPTURE REFERENCE

Ephesians 6:11 Amplified Bible, Classic
[11] Put on God's whole armor [the armor of a heavy-armed soldier which God supplies], that you may be able successfully to stand up against [all] the strategies *and* the deceits of the devil.

TO BE FILLED WITH THE HOLY SPIRIT

Father, I want to be filled with the Holy Spirit and speak in tongues. I understand that I will receive power to be victorious and tell others about your goodness. You said all I have to do is ask and I will receive. So, I ask You now, fill me with Your Spirit, I receive and speak NOW. (SPEAK NOW)
In Jesus Name! Amen.

SCRIPTURE REFERENCE:
Acts1:8 New International Version
[8] But you will receive power when the Holy Spirit comes on you; and you will be my witnesses in Jerusalem, and in all Judea and Samaria, and to the ends of the earth."
Acts 2:4 New International Version
[4] All of them were filled with the Holy Spirit and began to speak in other tongues[a] as the Spirit enabled them.

FOR A LIFE WELL PLEASING TO GOD

Father, the word says that without faith it is impossible to please You. I choose to believe that You are real; I choose to believe Your word and trust the leading of the Holy Spirit. Therefore, I say, not my will, but thy will be done in me Lord, today and every day. I choose to walk by faith today, pleasing You, making it my lifestyle and enjoy the benefits and rewards of walking by faith.
In Jesus Name! Amen.

SCRIPTURE REFERENCE:
Hebrews 11:6 Amplified Bible Classic
⁶ But without faith it is impossible to please *and* be satisfactory to Him. For whoever would come near to God must [necessarily] believe that God exists and that He is the rewarder of those who earnestly *and* diligently seek Him [out].

INNER PEACE

Father, I thank for Peace: the Peace that passes all understanding which guards my heart and calms my mind; that sustains and leads me. The Peace that You give, the world can't take it away. The Peace that delivers and strengthens my soul when the Enemy strikes a battle against me. I thank You that as I keep my mind stayed on You, I am kept in perfect Peace.
In Jesus Name! Amen.

SCRIPTURE REFERENCE:

Philippians 4:7 The Voice
[7] And know that the peace of God (*a peace* that is beyond any and all of our *human* understanding) will stand watch over your hearts and minds in Jesus, the Anointed One.

BE NOT WEARY IN WELL DOING

Father, I thank You for the strength to do all the works You have called me to do. I say I can do all things through Christ who gives me the strength. Nothing is too difficult for You, therefore, nothing is too difficult for me. You Have qualified and equipped me to be a blessing in my home, on my job and in my community. My help comes from the Lord, therefore, I say I am strong in You and the power of Your might. I never give up, quit or shrink back from purpose.

In Jesus Name! Amen.

SCRIPTURE REFERENCE:

Galatians 6:9 Amplified Bible

[9] Let us not grow weary *or* become discouraged in doing good, for at the proper time we will reap, if we do not give in.

PHYSICAL HEALING

Father, I thank You that I'm already healed, that's my story and I'm sticking to it. Your word says I am healed and I believe it. No matter what it looks like, feels like or what the doctor says, I agree with Your word, I believe Your report. By Your stripes I'm healed. His body was broken for my healing. Therefore, I say that the healing that Your word says is already mine shall surely manifest and be seen.

In Jesus Name! Amen.

SCRIPTURE REFERENCE:

Isaiah 53:5 Amplified Bible, Classic Edition

[5] But He was wounded for our transgressions, He was bruised for our guilt *and* iniquities; the chastisement [needful to obtain] peace *and* well-being for us was upon Him, and with the stripes [that wounded] Him we are healed *and* made whole.

STRENGTH

Father, I thank You for whenever I feel weak, I will say that I am strong in You. In Your presence is fullness of joy and Your joy is my strength, therefore I can do all things. Nothing is too difficult for You so nothing is too difficult for me. You are my strong tower, my anchor in the storm. I say that I am strong in You and in the power of Your Might. You are my strength so I have nothing to fear. **In Jesus Name! Amen.**

SCRIPTURE REFERENCE:

Psalm 46:1 Amplified Bible, Classic Edition

[1] God is our Refuge and Strength [mighty *and* impenetrable to temptation], a very present *and* well-proved help in trouble.

PROTECTION

Father, I thank You for giving Your angles charge over me to protect me, to keep me and deliver me from all hurt, harm, danger, injury or accident. I thank You for protecting me, You are a shield for me, You hide me under the shadow of Your wings. I thank You that I am covered by the Blood of Jesus and no weapon formed against me shall ever prosper. You are my strong tower, I run to You and I am kept safe.
In Jesus Name! Amen.

SCRIPTURE REFERENCE:

Psalm 91:4 Easy-to-Read Version

[4] You can go to him for protection. He will cover you like a bird spreading its wings over its babies. You can trust him to surround and protect you like a shield.

WISDOM

Father, I thank You for wisdom today, wisdom that is pure, with no hidden agenda, that expresses itself thru mercy, kindness, sincerity; the wisdom that gives me peace to know that what I am about to say and do is what is right. I thank You that wisdom from You enables me to respond adequately in every situation. I walk after the Spirit and I have the mind of Christ. Therefore, I say ALL is well, ALL things are working together for good.
In Jesus Name! Amen.

SCRIPTURE REFERENCE:

James 3:17 New International Version

[17] But the wisdom that comes from heaven is first of all pure; then peace-loving, considerate, submissive, full of mercy and good fruit, impartial and sincere.

PROSPERTIY - ALL MY NEEDS MET

Father, I thank You that by faith, all my needs are met. Your word says that You give seed to the sower and multiply the seed sown. I am a sower, therefore, I am a reaper. I thank You then, for multiplied seed. I give and it is given unto me, pressed down, shaken together and running over. I have more than enough. I am able to abound toward every good work. Thank You for blessing all the works of my hands.

In Jesus Name! Amen.

SCRIPTURE REFERENCE

Luke 6:38 King James

"Give, and it will be given to you. Good measure, pressed down, shaken together, running over…

2 Corinthians 9:10a Amplified Bible

[0] Now He who provides seed for the sower and bread for food will provide and multiply your seed for sowing [that is, your resources]…

TO BE DEBT FREE

Father, today I declare my freedom from debt. You said I am to owe no man nothing but love. I say I can do all things through Your strength. I say that I am disciplined, focus and I on purpose shall live within my means. I will not allow myself to be a slave to overspending but rather embrace saving, investing and avenues of increase. I choose to be a producer and not a consumer, I thank You for ways to make my money work for me so I won't have to work so hard for it. I see myself debt free.
In Jesus Name! Amen.

SCRIPTURE REFERENCE:
Romans 13:8 Common English Bible
[8] Don't be in debt to anyone, except for the 6obligation to love each other. Whoever loves another person has fulfilled the Law
Proverbs 22:7 King James Version
The rich ruleth over the poor, and the borrower is servant to the lender

FOR A NEW HOME

Father, I thank that because I delight myself in You, my heart's desire for a new home is granted. I thank You that the home You have for me, by faith, is already mine. I'm searching for my home and it's waiting for me. I thank for a home in an area that I love and with good neighbors. I thank You for a favored deal and it even being debt free. I thank You that my new home has: SAY AND/ OR WRITE DOWN WHAT YOU WANT YOUR HOME TO HAVE AND LOOK LIKE.
In Jesus Name! Amen.

SCRIPTURE REFERENCE:

Psalm 37:4 King James Version
[4] Delight thyself also in the LORD: and he shall give thee the desires of thine heart.

VICTORY OVER FEAR

Father, I thank You for giving me the spirit of love, power and a sound mind. Therefore, tranquility, being well balanced, disciplined and self- controlled is my portion. Your perfect love casts out all fear and every feeling and emotion attached to it. Even though fear may be present, it has no place in me for Your Presence is greater. I am ready, willing, eager and happy to obey Your will.
In Jesus Name! Amen.

SCRIPTURE REFERENCE:
II Timothy 1:7 Amplified Bible, Classic Edition
[7] For God did not give us a spirit of timidity (of cowardice, of craven and cringing and fawning fear), but [He has given us a spirit] of power and of love and of calm *and* well-balanced mind *and* discipline *and* self-control.

VICTORY OVER ANXIETY

Father, when I praise You, my soul is uplifted, encouraged, given hope and renewed. When I anxious or stressed out, I will remember to think about things that are lovely, pure, honest, just, praise worthy, of a good report and virtuous. In Your Presence I'm reminded of who I am, what I can do and what I have in You. I will always believe the report of the Lord which says all things are always working together for my good. Therefore, anxiety has no place in me.
In Jesus Name! Amen.

SCRIPTURE RFERENCE:
Proverbs 12:25 New English Translation
[25] A person's anxiety weighs down his heart, but an appropriate word is encouraging.

DELIVERANCE

Father, I thank You for the Anointing that breaks every chain and destroys every yoke of bondage. You said let the redeemed say so. Therefore, I say I am free from _____ this day! Your Spirit is in me and where Your Spirit is there is liberty so I choose to stand in the victory that purchased my freedom. For He whom the Son sets free is free indeed. I am Your child and I AM FREE! I believe it! I stand on it! And I will not be moved from it! I am delivered!

In Jesus Name! Amen.

SCRIPTURE REFERENCE:

John 8:36 Authorized (King James) Version
[36] If the Son, therefore,
shall make you free, ye shall be free indeed.

DEPRESSION - SUICIDAL THOUGHTS

Father, Your word says that a merry heart is good like a medicine, so I will think myself happy. When depression comes, I can put my hope in You and bless Your name. Depression is temporary but suicide is a permanent solution and to that I say NO! My life is valuable and I am enough. I am loved, forgiven and redeemed. Goodness and mercy follow me, Peace keeps me, Your strength sustains, and Your Grace is sufficient. So, I choose life. **In Jesus Name! Amen.**

SCRIPTURE REFERENCE

Psalm 42:5-6a New International Version
Why, my soul, are you downcast? Why so disturbed within me? Put your hope in God, for I will yet praise him, my Savior and my God.
⁶ My soul is downcast within me; therefore, I will remember you…

VICTORY OVER PROCRASTINATION

Father, I thank You for the grace that's on my life to do everything I need to do for You, myself, my family, my church/ ministry, my career and others. By faith, I choose to actively pursue Your purpose and plan for my life, use my time wisely, organize, prioritize, be intentional, purposeful, disciplined, productive and finish what I start.
In Jesus Name! Amen.

SCRIPTURE REFERENCE
James 4:17 New Living Translation
[17] Remember, it is sin to know what you ought to do and then not do it.
1 Corinthians 14:40 New International Version
[40] But everything should be done in a fitting and orderly way.

VICTORY OVER GRIEF

Father, when my heart is heavy, You said to put on the garment of praise to dismiss the spirit of heaviness. So, I praise You now! When overwhelming sadness, and anxiety, are present, I give You praise. When sorrow: feelings of loss, guilt, remorse and regret grip me, I will praise You some more. Father, I cast those feelings on you and thank You for Your mercy, patience, love and kindness toward me. Father, I thank You for wrapping your loving arms around me when it seems like I can't make it but You always assure me that I can and I will.

In Jesus Name! Amen.

SCRIPTURE REFERENCE:

Isaiah 53:4 The Living Bible

[4] Yet it was *our* grief he bore, *our* sorrows that weighed him down. And we thought his troubles were a punishment from God, for his *own* sins!

VICTORY OVER SEXUAL IMPURITY

Father, Like Adam and Eve, You created me to have and enjoy sex with my spouse. Therefore, I renounce all sexual activities outside of marriage for solitary pleasure or in unison with one or more persons. I put away all devices, media influences, phone conversations, magazines, establishments, ungodly relationships, and all sexually perverse, stimuli and ask You to forgive me. By faith, I turn away from what once had me bound.
In Jesus Name! Amen.

SCRIPTURE REFERENCE:
I Thessalonians 4:3-5 Common English Bible
3 God's will is that your lives are dedicated to him.[a] This means that you stay away from sexual immorality 4 and learn how to control your own body in a pure[b] and respectable way. 5 Don't be controlled by your sexual urges like the Gentiles who don't know God.

VICTORY OVER ADULTERY

Father, I ask You to forgive me for committing the sin of adultery, for having a sexual relationship with someone outside of my marriage. I make a choice to repent and turn away from the act and the person(s) I have entered into sin with. I thank You for the strength (that comes from spending time with God) to overcome this relationship and everything that comes with it. I put a guard on my ear and eye gates as I walk closer with You. I choose to honor You in my marriage, my spouse and my body from this day forward.

In Jesus Name! Amen.

SCRIPTURE REFERENCE:

1 Corinthians 7:2 Easy to Read Version

2 But sexual sin is a danger, so each man should enjoy his own wife, and each woman should enjoy her own husband.

VICTORY OVER FORNICATION

Father, I ask You to forgive me for committing the sin of fornication, for having a sexual relationship with someone I'm not married to. I make a choice to repent and turn away from the act and the person(s) I have entered into sin with. I choose to remain celibate until marriage. I thank You for the strength (that comes from spending time with God) to overcome this relationship and everything that comes with it. I break all soul ties. I choose to honor You, my singleness and my body from this day forward.

In Jesus Name! Amen.

SCRIPTURE REFERENCE:
1 Corinthians 6:18 Authorized King James
[18] Flee fornication. Every sin that a man doeth is without the body; but he that committeth fornication sinneth against his own body.

VICTORY OVER AFFLICTION-HARDSHIPS

Father, Your word say that I am delivered from any and all affliction, and the stress caused by hardships. So today I agree with You and I declare my victory, freedom and deliverance from (**NAME IT/ THEM).** I say, by faith, that all my needs are already met, every crooked place has been made straight and no weapon formed against me can ever prosper. I thank You for the strength to endure and joy, peace and to face each day. I am more than a conqueror.

In Jesus Name! Amen.

SCRIPTURE REFERENCE:

Psalms 34:19 Amplified Bible

¹⁹ Many hardships *and* perplexing circumstances confront the righteous, But the LORD rescues him from them all.

OVER DRUG & ALCOHOL ADDICTION

Father, Your word says that no temptation can over take me, or make me stumble and fall. Therefore, I boldly declare that I am delivered from **SAY WHAT YOU'RE DELIVERED FROM.** I have victory over it/them. I am an overcomer, more than a conqueror, victorious and free! Your Spirit is in me and I stand in the liberty that made me free. **In Jesus Name! Amen.**

SCRIPTURE REFERENCE:

1 Corinthians 10:13 English Standard Version

[13] No temptation has overtaken you that is not common to man. God is faithful, and he will not let you be tempted beyond your ability, but with the temptation he will also provide the way of escape, that you may be able to endure it.

BUSINESS/ ENTREPRENUERIAL SUCCESS

Father, I thank for blessing the works of my hands, for favor in business. I thank You that all things are being added to me because I put You first. I thank You for showing me what to sell and what to buy for profit, who to consult with and seek out as a mentor(s); what books to read and if necessary, what educational level to pursue. I thank You for giving me the power to get wealth and for discernment in all business deals.

In Jesus Name! Amen.

SCRIPTURE REFERENCE

Luke 16:10a Common English Bible

[10] "Whoever is faithful with little is also faithful with much…

Deuteronomy 8:18a King James Version

[18] But thou shalt remember the LORD thy God: for it is he that giveth thee power to get wealth…

MY BOSS – SUPERVISOR

Father, I thank You for **YOUR WORKPLACE** the job You blessed me with as a resource and for **YOUR BOSS/ SUPERVISOR.** Father because I know that You are my Source, I purpose to work there and do my best, to work as unto You. I will always respect, honor and obey him/her because I am serving you and not them. So Father I ask you to bless him/her with peace, strength and wisdom so he/she can be on top of their game not ruling harshly but fairly without favoritism or fear. **In Jesus Name! Amen**

SCRIPTURE REFERENCE
Ephesians 6:5-8 The Message
5-8 Servants, respectfully obey your earthly masters but always with an eye to obeying the *real* master, Christ. Don't just do what you have to do to get by, but work heartily, as Christ's servants doing what God wants you to do.

PRAYER for STAFF and/or EMPLOYEES

Father, I thank You that since I have been faithful over a little you have blessed me to be ruler over much in a position of leadership. Therefore, I pray for those under my leadership that they would have peace in their homes, restful sleep at night, bodies free from sickness, hearts filled with goodness and minds filled with focus for each days' tasks in their homes, at work and during their times of recreation. I thank for the strength to be fair, kind and lead as if I am serving unto You.

In Jesus Name! Amen.

SCRIPTURE REFERENCE

Leviticus 25:43 Amplified Bible, Classic Edition

[43] You shall not rule over him with harshness (severity, oppression), but you shall [reverently] fear your God.

CO-WORKERS

Father, I thank You for the people I work with, some are like family and all are valuable to You. God, I pray Your favor be upon them, establish the works of their hands that they would be fruitful in all that they do. I pray that they be an asset to the company and not a detriment. That they do their work in excellence as unto You. I pray that they have peace in their hearts, minds and homes. That all their needs are met and that they are kept safe as they come and go. Most of all I pray that any that don't know You would seek to know You and see Your light in me.

In Jesus Name! Amen.

SCRIPTURE REFERENCE
Psalm 90:17 Living Bible

[17] and let the Lord our God favor us and give us success. May he give permanence to all we do.

PROMOTION

Father, You said that my gift would make room for me and bring me before great men. Therefore, I thank You that my name is being spoken in rooms that I know not of. I have sat at Your feet and grown in wisdom and matured in natural and spiritual things. So I boldly declare that I am next in line for a miracle, for the promotion that I desire. I am called by You and qualified. I have labored and shown myself approved before God and man. Lord, I thank You in advance for my promotion.
In Jesus Name! Amen.

SCRIPTURE REFERENCE
Proverbs 22:29 Tree of Life Version
[29] Do you see a man skilled in his work He will stand before kings. He will not stand before obscure people.

YOUR PASTOR(S)

Father, I lift up my Pastor and all Pastors. I thank You that he/she is led by Your Spirit and is a doer of Your word. He/she is an epistle fit to be read of those they come in contact with. He/ she spends time in the word and prayer and lives a life well pleasing to You. I thank You that he/ she is sober temperate, given to hospitality, blameless and a good steward of church finances, is orderly, well respected and respectable.

In Jesus Name! Amen

SCRIPTURE REFERENCE

I Tim. 3:2-4 The Living Bible

[2] For a pastor must be a good man whose life cannot be spoken against. He must have only one wife, and he must be hard working and thoughtful, orderly, and full of good deeds... [3] He must not be a drinker or quarrelsome, but he must be gentle and kind and not be one who loves money.

THE BODY OF CHRIST

Father, I thank You that no denomination can separate the Body of Christ. By faith we come into the full knowledge of who You are. I Thank You for believers who are fruitful unto every good work, walk uprightly before You, who win souls, who are intercessors, do good and not evil, who are peace keepers, unified and fitly joined together, increasing in love.
In Jesus Name! Amen.

SCRIPTURE REFERENCE
Ephesians 4:16 Amplified Bible
[16] From Him the whole body [the church, in all its various parts], joined and knitted *firmly* together by what every joint supplies, when each part is working properly, causes the body to grow *and* mature, building itself up [a]in [unselfish] love.

CHURCH LEADERSHIP

Father, today I lift up all Pastors, Prophets, Apostles, Teachers and Evangelists. Deacons, Elders, Overseers and Bishops. I thank You that as they pour out to the Body of Christ, that You will pour into them the abundance of peace revelation, strength, wisdom and financial blessings to do all the works you've called them to do. May they be above reproach, always remember that Your grace is sufficient and be not weary in well doing. **In Jesus Name! Amen.**

SCRIPTURE RFERENCE
Ephesians 4:11-12 King James Version
[11] And he gave some, apostles; and some, prophets; and some, evangelists; and some, pastors and teachers; [12] For the perfecting of the saints, for the work of the ministry, for the edifying of the body of Christ:

HELPS MINISTRY

Father, today I lift up Helps Ministries: Ushers, Greeters, Praise Teams, Choirs, Children and Youth Ministries, and all others that help to do the work of the ministry. I pray that each member is Submitted to God, their Pastor and ministry leader, given to prayer, Spirit led, appointed and anointed, faithful to the ministry, lives a Godly life and is a doer of the word so that the kingdom of God can grow, the word can have free course and God shall be glorified.
In Jesus Name! Amen.

SCRIPTURE REFERENCE
Acts 6:3 Amplified Bible
[3] Wherefore, brethren, look ye out among you seven men of honest report, full of the Holy Ghost and wisdom, whom we may appoint over this business.

HAVE A HEART FOR THE LOST

Father, I thank You for giving me the heart of a Soul Winner. You said soul winning is wise and that no one is excused from the service of reconciling men and women to Christ. For You would have everyone to be saved and come into the full knowledge of the truth. Therefore, without fear or hesitation I say You can depend on me Lord to tell others about You.
In Jesus Name! Amen.

SCRIPTURE REFERENCE
Proverbs 11:30 Amplified Bible
The fruit of the [consistently] righteous is a tree of life, And he who is wise captures *and* wins souls [for God—he gathers them for eternity].

BE RESTORED TO CHRIST

Father, forgive me for I have sinned, AGAIN! I thank You for never turning me away. I thank You for grace, mercy and unconditional love that draws me back every time I go astray. This time, I repent and turn away from thoughts that produce sin in my life. I will now use my weapons and say I am free. For where Your Spirit is, there is freedom. **In Jesus Name! Amen.**

SCRIPTURE REFERENCE

1 John 1:9 King James Version

[9] If we confess our sins, he is faithful and just to forgive us our sins, and to cleanse us from all unrighteousness.

Acts 8:22 King James Version

[22] Repent therefore of this thy wickedness, and pray God, if perhaps the thought of thine heart may be forgiven thee.

GOVERNMENT LEADERS

Father, I pray for Kings, Presidents, U.S. Congress Persons, Governors, Mayors, City Council Persons, and all who sit in seats of governance. I pray that if any don't know You that You would send laborers across their path. I pray that they would govern justly, fairly and with wisdom, that they would seek Godly council before decisions are made or a bill is voted on.

In Jesus Name! Amen.

SCRIPTURE REFERENCE

I Timothy 2:1-2 New King James Version (NKJV) Therefore I [a]exhort first of all that supplications, prayers, intercessions, *and* giving of thanks be made for all men, **²** for kings and all who are in [b]authority, that we may lead a quiet and peaceable life in all godliness and [c]reverence.

ALL IN POSITIONS OF AUTHORITY

Father, because the structure of authority is set up by You, I pray for all who hold administrative and managerial positions who are responsible for decision making in any area of life. I pray that they would rule with integrity, impartiality and wisdom, that they realize they are in Your service. May those under their authority realize that they too are in Your service and not be in rebellion to authority. I pray any that don't know You, would seek You. I especially pray for **NAME(S)** so that Your will be done in, through and for them.
In Jesus Name! Amen.

SCRIPTURE REFERENCE
Romans 13:1 The Voice
It is important that all of us submit to the authorities who have charge over us because God establishes all authority *in heaven and on the earth*.

FOR ALL MEN & WOMEN

Father, because it is Your desire that everyone receives salvation, I pray for men and women everywhere, for those don't know You. I ask that You would send forth laborers across their path to minister Your life and Love to them so that they would want to be saved and receive the benefits of the newness of life. I thank You Lord for bringing them to place where they can make a sane decision to accept Jesus as Lord, and Christ be formed in them.

In Jesus Name! Amen.

SCRIPTURE REFERENCE

I Timothy 2:1,4 New King James Version

1Therefore I [a]exhort first of all that supplications, prayers, intercessions, *and* giving of thanks be made for all men, 4 who desires all men to be saved and to come to the knowledge of the truth.

YOUR CITY – STATE

Father, I pray over every state, region, county, city, ward and neighborhood. I pray for peace in our streets, jobs would be plentiful, crime would be at an all-time low, an end to gun violence, our children would be safe in their schools, people would find solace in prayer, friends and family rather than drugs and alcohol. I pray for programs for the mentally, shelter for the homeless and family relationships be restored.
In Jesus Name! Amen.

SCRIPTURE REFERENCE
Jeremiah 29:7-11 King James Version
[7] And seek the peace of the city whither I have caused you to be carried away captives, and pray unto the LORD for it: for in the peace thereof shall ye have peace.
Joshua 6:16b King James Version
...Shout; for the LORD hath given you the city.

FOR EDUCATORS – SCHOOL SYSTEMS

Father, I thank You for all those who work in our nation's schools, especially **NAME or ORG**. I ask You to give them wisdom to teach children who present daily challenges, be creative and teach in new ways, courage to face each day, renewed passion for their purpose and compassion for students who struggle to learn. I pray that they daily be enveloped in Your Peace, that they do what's necessary to facilitate good health and life balance. I pray they never forget their value and are valued by the families of the children they teach.
In Jesus Name! Amen.

SCRIPTURE REFERENCE

Philippians 4:19 King James Version
[19] But my God shall supply all your need according to his riches in glory by Christ Jesus.

FIRST RESPONDERS

Father, I lift up our First Responders. I thank You for keeping them safe from all hurt, harm, danger, injury or accident as they keep us safe. Thank You for giving Your Angels charge over them Lord. Give them peaceful sleep and rest in their souls, erasing painful memories of things they've had to see and endure. Bless what they have willingly put their hands to as they serve their community without fear or regret.
In Jesus Name! Amen.

SCRIPTURE REFERENCE
Psalm 91:10-11 Amplified Bible Classic Edition
[10] There shall no evil befall you, nor any plague *or* calamity come near your tent.[11] For He will give His angels [especial] charge over you to accompany *and* defend *and* preserve you in all your ways [of obedience and service].

VICTORY IN MARRIAGE

Father, I thank You for the life partner You chose for me. I will love, honor and cherish **NAME** as long as I live, in good times and bad, in sickness and health, whether rich or poor. I will see to **NAME** needs before my own, apologize even if I'm right so the relationship can win. I will not go to bed angry, fall out over money nor withhold sex as a form of punishment and listen to understand. **In Jesus Name! Amen.**

SCRIPTURE REFERENCE

Matthew 19:4-5 New Living Translation

4 "Haven't you read the Scriptures?" Jesus replied. "They record that from the beginning 'God made them male and female.'[a]" 5 And he said, "'This explains why a man leaves his father and mother and is joined to his wife, and the two are united into one.'[b]

HUSBAND'S PRAYER FOR HIS WIFE

Father, I thank You for my wife, created just for me. I thank You for helping me to communicate effectively with her and dwell with her according to knowledge. She is my good thing. My prayers are heard and my life is blessed because of her. Thank You for showing me how to treat her as the Queen that she is. No other woman compares for my eyes and my heart belong to her. I support her in all that she does. I pray that everything she puts her hands to prospers and I vow to support her dreams **In Jesus Name! Amen.**

SCRIPTURE REFERENCE

Peter 3:7 King James Version

[7] Likewise, ye husbands, dwell with them according to knowledge, giving honor unto the wife, as unto the weaker vessel, and as being heirs together of the grace of life; that your prayers be not hindered.

PRAYER TO BE A GOOD HUSBAND

Father, I thank You for my wife, my gift. I purpose to love her as Christ loved the Church and gave Himself for Her. He gave Himself so His Bride could be healed, whole, saved, safe, all her needs met and be at peace. Therefore, just as Christ is to the church I will be to my wife. I will put her first, cherish her and honor her.
In Jesus Name! Amen.

SCRIPTURE REFERENCE
Ephesians 5:25,28-29 New International Version
[25] Husbands, love your wives, just as Christ loved the church and gave himself up for her [28] In this same way, husbands ought to love their wives as their own bodies. He who loves his wife loves himself. [29] After all, no one ever hated their own body, but they feed and care for their body, just as Christ does the church—

WIFE'S PRAYER FOR HER HUSBAND

Father, I thank you for my husband, my King, lover and friend. I thank You that he is, wise, strong, kind intelligent, honest, gentle, righteous and prayerful and studies Your word. Father, You are first in his life. He provides for me, puts my needs above his own and takes care of home. Lord, I thank You for surrounding him with favor, watching over him, giving him the power to get wealth and granting his hearts desires.
In Jesus Name! Amen.

SCRIPTURE REFERENCE
Song of Solomon 5:16a New Living Translation
[16] His mouth is sweetness itself he is desirable in every way. Such, O women of Jerusalem, is my lover, my friend.

TO BE A GOOD WIFE

Father, I desire to be the best wife I can be for my husband. I was made for him. I am the crown he wears, I am submitted, loving, and a good steward with money. I am not given to arguing but seek to communicate effectively. I bring him no shame and his heart safely trusts in me. I am his good thing, his help meet, suitable for him, to help him fulfill his purpose. He is happy to dwell with me in peace. **In Jesus name! Amen.**

SCRIPTURE REFERENCE

Ephesians 5:22-33 New International Version
[22] Wives, submit yourselves to your own husbands as you do to the Lord. [23] For the husband is the head of the wife as Christ is the head of the church, his body, of which he is the Savior. [24] Now as the church submits to Christ, so also wives should submit to their husbands in everything.

CHILDREN – ALL CHILDREN - ALL AGES

Father, I thank You for my child(ren), for all children. They are Your inheritance and reward. They are/were only on loan to us to train them in Your ways. I pray that they know they are loved and love themselves. They are blessed going in and out, blessed in the city and the field. I thank You for giving Your angels charge over them to keep and deliver them from all hurt, harm, danger, injury or accident. They are redeemed of the lord and no weapon formed against them shall prosper. Your blood covers them and by Your stripes they are healed. By faith, they have separated themselves and come out from among all ungodliness, they do not indulge in activities that are not like You. They are saved, sanctified and with Your Holy Spirit. They are not unequally yoked with unbelievers, but rather fellowship with those of like precious faith. They pressure their peers to do good and not evil. I thank You that they hear Your voice and the voice of a stranger they'll not follow. They are submitted

71

to God and therefore submit themselves to all authority. They don't use foul language but only that which ministers grace. Their purpose is great and shall not be hindered, denied, delayed or aborted but shall be fulfilled. I curse at the root and command to die and dry up: every ungodly soul tie, evil association, ungodly acquaintance unholy connection and demonic influence, Devil, your assignment is hereby dismissed. Great is the Peace of my children. They are an asset to society, everything they put their hands to shall prosper and they will, shall and continue to do great things, walking uprightly before You while they live. They honor their parent(s) and all shall go well for them. **In Jesus Name! Amen.**

SCRIPTURE REFERENCE

Psalm 127:3-5 New Living Translation

[3] Children are a gift from the LORD;
  they are a reward from him.

PARENTS

Father, I thank you for watching over my parent(s), keeping ____ safe and satisfying ____ with a long life, I thank you Lord for keeping ____ strong, their bodies healed and their minds whole, that ____ may have and enjoy the good life so that their joy be full. I ask that You bless ____ abundantly with everything they have need of and grant their hearts desires and I thank You for doing so.
In Jesus Name! Amen.

SCRIPTUR REFERENCE

Deuteronomy 5:16 Easy-to-Read Version

[16] 'You must honor your father and your mother. The LORD your God has commanded you to do this. If you follow this command, you will live a long time, and everything will go well for you in the land that the LORD your God gives you.

EXTENDED FAMILY

Father, thank You for the gift of family. My aunties, uncles, cousins, siblings, in-laws and family friends, especially **NAME(S)**. I pray that those who know You would remain steadfast in the faith and any that don't know You would seek You. I thank You for family unity and love and that our bond is never broken. May they be blessed with strong healthy minds and bodies even as their souls prosper. I ask You to watch over them, protect them, and bless them with long life. I pray that all disagreements be resolved, debts forgiven and relationships restored. **In Jesus name! Amen.**

Ephesians 3:14-15 King James Version
[14] For this cause I bow my knees unto the Father of our Lord Jesus Christ, [15] Of whom the whole family in heaven and earth is named,

TO WALK IN LOVE

Father, I thank You for allowing me entrance into Your presence. There I become more like You. Spending time with You makes it easy to love You, myself and others. I am accepted and perfected in Your love. Love casts out fear and covers a multitude of sin. Christ died for me out of love. Therefore, I chose to die to self and walk in love, my faith won't work without it. I can't please You if I don't walk by faith. Love is the more excellent way.

In Jesus Name! Amen.

SCRIPTURE REFERENCE

Galatians 5:6 The Message

For in Christ, neither our most conscientious religion nor disregard of religion amounts to anything. What matters is something far more interior: faith expressed in love.

TO FORGIVE

Father, I choose to forgive. I Thank You for helping me understand that forgiveness is not a feeling but a choice that I consciously make. So, no matter how I feel about a person or what they've done, I will and do forgive because I want to be forgiven and I trust that my feelings will soon agree with my choice. (WHEN YOU FEEL LIKE YOU HAVEN'T OR CAN'T FORGIVE, REMEMBER THE CHOICE YOU MADE AND SPEAK FAITH).
In Jesus Name! Amen.

SCRIPTURE REFERENCE
Matthew 6:14-15 The Living Bible
[14]Your heavenly Father will forgive you if you forgive those who sin against you; [15] but if you if *you* refuse to forgive *them, he* will not forgive *you.*

TO MARRY A GODLY SPOUSE

Father, I believe my desire to be married is a Godly desire. Therefore, I thank You for a life partner who puts You first, is given to prayer and study of the word, believes in the Trinity, believes that husbands should love their wives like Christ loves the church and that wives should submit to their husbands; has good credit, attends church regularly and sufficient income. We shall be equally yoked together and enjoy our lives in unity. I thank You for helping me to make myself ready to receive. We two shall become one.
In Jesus Name! Amen.

SCRIPTURE REFERENCE
Psalm 37:4 Amplified Bible, Classic Edition
[4] Delight yourself also in the Lord, and He will give you the desires *and* secret petitions of your heart.

ENJOY BEING SINGLE

Father, I Thank You for I am blessed beyond measure as a single person. I am in love with You and I am in love with me. My cup runs over. I delight in the way that You have set forth before me. My steps have been ordered by You and for that I am grateful. Even though I am alone, I am not lonely for You are with me, my life is full and I am content. I celebrate being single. **In Jesus Name! Amen.**

SCRIPTURE REFERENCE
John 15:9 Amplified Bible, Classic Edition
[9] I have loved you, [just] as the Father has loved Me; abide in My love [[a]continue in His love with Me].

Author Biography

Due to the circumstances of her life, having a child at 13, drug use, promiscuity, and more, Toy came to understand, she had a need that only God could meet. As a young Christian, who didn't grow up in church, she quickly realized the need for prayer but she didn't know how to pray. So she bought a prayer book and daily prayed every prayer in that book. Never knowing that she was sowing seeds that would one day reap a harvest. That harvest being helping others in prayer the same way she was helped, with a prayer book. This is her fifth book. As you commit to daily prayer, you will be blessed beyond measure. You can rest assured that every prayer in this book is based on God's Word and they will be answered. So, pray every day and get ready to receive what you are believing for.

More **I CAN HAVE WHAT I SAY** prayer books:

My Healing Scriptures and Confessions

Everyday Prayers for Young Adults

Everyday Prayers for Teens

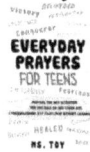

The Struggle Was Real …Until I Said It Was Over

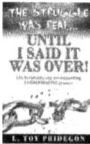

For order information, leave a review or to see our other products go to:
icanhavewhatisay.com
Feel free to email your prayer request to:
icanhavewhatisay@gmail.com

I'm Praying for You!
Sincerely L. Toy Pridegon

www.ingramcontent.com/pod-product-compliance
Lightning Source LLC
Chambersburg PA
CBHW071140280326
41935CB00010B/1300